AR

Book Level = 6.0

Points = 1.0

DISASTER!
FIRE

Jason Hook

RAINTREE
STECK-VAUGHN
RSVP PUBLISHERS

A Harcourt Company

Austin   New York
www.raintreesteckvaughn.com

LOOK FOR THE FLAMES

Look for the flames in boxes like this. Here you will find extra facts, stories, and other interesting information about fire disasters.

Published by Raintree Steck-Vaughn Publishers,
an imprint of Steck-Vaughn Company.

Library of Congress Cataloging-in-Publication Data

Designer: Victoria Webb
Editor: Kate Phelps
Picture Research: Lynda Lines

ISBN 0-7398-6314-2

Printed in Taiwan   Bound in United States
1 2 3 4 5 6 7 8 9 0 LB 06 05 04 03 02

Acknowledgments
We wish to thank the following individuals and organizations for their assistance and for supplying material from their collections: Ancient Art and Architecture Collection 6 (Ronald Sheridan), 6-7, 13 top; Art Archive 13 top (Dagli Orti); Associated Press 9 (Rob Griffith), 11 bottom, 18 bottom, 19 bottom, 22 (Pat Sullivan), 23, 31 (Alan Solomon); Bridgeman Art Library 26 (Hubert Robert); Corbis 4 bottom (Gianni Dagli Orti), 5 (Bettmann), 10 (Bettmann), 11 top (Bettmann), 12 (Bettman), 16 top (Hulton Deutsch), 16 bottom (Bettmann), 18 top (Bettmann), 27 (Bettmann), 28 (Historical Picture Archive), 30 (Bettmann); Digital Vision 29; Hulton Archive 14-15, 15 top; Mary Evans Picture Library 19 top; Rex Features 2 (Ian Prince), 3, 4 top (Mansell/Timepix), 8, 20 (Sipa/Nicol), 21 top (Today/Geoff Bollands), 21 bottom (Ian Prince), 24 bottom (Sipa/Gelin); Topham Picturepoint 1 (AP), 7, 9, 17, 24 top (Imageworks/John Maier Jr), 25.

◀ In March 1991, fire blazes from oil wells in Kuwait.

CONTENTS

▶ *A bush fire rages out of control in Australia.*

FIRE!

The discovery of fire in prehistoric times totally changed the way humans lived. Fire brought with it heat and light. But when humans started building towns of wooden houses, fire sometimes brought something else—disaster.

▲ *The Great Fire of London, in 1666, was so fierce that people had to escape across the Thames River in boats.*

Throughout history, fires have destroyed towns and cities. Some have been started by people. London burned down in 1666 because a careless baker forgot to cover the ashes in his oven. Other fires are natural disasters. When an earthquake struck Tokyo in 1923, it started fires that killed over 140,000 people.

◄ *This mosaic shows a hero named Prometheus. Stories from Ancient Greece tell how Prometheus stole fire from the gods and gave it to humans.*

▲ *People flee from Tokyo in 1923, after an earthquake shattered the city and started a number of terrible fires.*

Even today, fire can affect entire countries. In 1997, there was a drought in Indonesia. When farmers began burning trees to clear some land, their fires raged out of control. The blaze lasted ten months and destroyed a vast area of rain forest. It hid Indonesia beneath a cloud of smoke that blocked out the light of the sun.

FIRE AND BRIMSTONE

"The Lord rained upon Sodom and upon Gomorrah brimstone and fire." In this way, the Bible records one of the earliest fire disasters. Sodom and Gomorrah were real cities in the Middle East. Fire destroyed them around 1900 B.C., after an earthquake or possibly a meteor storm.

GREAT FIRE OF LONDON

During the early hours of Sunday, September 2, 1666, a fire began in a bakery in London's Pudding Lane. In the next four days, the flames reduced almost the whole of the city to ashes.

The blaze started in the home of Thomas Farynor, King Charles II's baker. It had been a hot, dry summer, and London's wooden houses caught fire easily. Flames spread quickly through the narrow streets, driven west by a strong wind. Thousands of people fled with their belongings to boats on the Thames River. Others, including the king himself, fought the fire with buckets of water.

▲ *The Great Fire sweeps through London. Flames leapt so high that pigeons fell burning from the sky.*

▼ *London Bridge was the scene of many fires. One of them, in 1633, destroyed shops including grocers, hat-makers, and glove-makers.*

In four days, the blaze destroyed 400 streets, 13,200 houses, and 87 churches. St. Paul's Cathedral was burned to the ground. Over 100,000 people were made homeless, yet only six lives were lost.

In the following years a new London was built, with wider streets and stone houses. Many buildings were designed by Sir Christopher Wren. They included a new St. Paul's, with the magnificent dome you can still see today.

▲ *In the 1600s, people fought fires with buckets of water and hand-pumps called "squirts."*

🔥 LONDON BRIDGE IS BURNING DOWN

On July 11, 1212, fire broke out at one end of London Bridge. As spectators gathered on the bridge, the flames suddenly swept past them. People leaped into the Thames to escape, and in the panic at least 3,000 died.

ASH WEDNESDAY FIRE

In Australia there are about 15,000 fires in the countryside, or bush, every year. Many are quite small. But on Ash Wednesday, February 16, 1983, the most terrible bush fire in history began.

▼ *Flames race across the Australian bush.*

After a long drought and in temperatures over 104 °F (40 °C), the bush was dry as a bone and caught fire easily. Australia's many eucalyptus trees spread the blaze quickly. Their oil-filled leaves turned into fireballs, which leapt across the treetops. Burning bark fluttered up to 19 miles (30 km) on the wind, and started new blazes. Soon, 180 different bush fires were burning across southern Australia.

GREAT BLACK DRAGON

Forest fires are the world's biggest blazes. In the summer of 1988, forest fires destroyed 720,000 acres (290,000 hectares) of Yellowstone National Park in Wyoming. In May 1987, the Great Black Dragon Fire in northern China raged for 21 days, scorching over one million acres (half a million hectares) and killing 193 people.

On Christmas 2001, bush fires again raged across Australia. Here, firefighters battle flames that have reached the outskirts of Sydney.

As the Ash Wednesday fires spread, people heard a roar like a train approaching. This was followed by the rattle of burning sticks falling like hail on their roofs. Then they saw enormous balls of fire racing toward them. Strong winds spread the flames at the terrifying speed of 100 miles per hour (160 km/h).

For two days, the bush fires raged. They lit up the night like daytime and darkened the day with smoke. Flames killed 200,000 sheep and cattle, and claimed the lives of 75 people.

Yellowstone National Park, left blackened and bare by forest fire.

JOELMA BUILDING

As cities become more crowded, people live and work in taller buildings. In these towering skyscrapers a small fire can quickly turn into a major disaster.

The Joelma Building in São Paulo, Brazil, was 25 stories high. On the morning of February 1, 1974, some 650 people were working there when a fire broke out on the 11th floor. The Joelma was built using material that caught fire easily, and the blaze soon raged through the building.

◀ *Smoke pours from the Joelma Building. The fire gave off such heat that it peeled paint from helicopters flown in to rescue people.*

BLAZING BUILDINGS

Fire can consume even the greatest of buildings. On the night of November 30, 1936, the Crystal Palace in London was destroyed by a blaze so big it was seen by a pilot flying over the English Channel. On July 9, 1994, fire raged through 700-year-old York Minster cathedral after it was struck by lightning.

People in the Joelma who were working on the floors above the blaze were trapped. Firefighters arrived, but their ladders were too short to reach the top stories. Rescue helicopters were driven back by the heat.

▶ Built in 1851, London's sparkling Crystal Palace was the world's first building of iron and glass. In 1936, fire reduced it to twisted wreckage.

▼ After fire had destroyed much of the roof of York Minster in 1994, firefighters fought for hours to save the rest of the cathedral.

The inferno in the Joelma reached a temperature of 1,292 °F (700 °C). Some people escaped to the roof, where they ran around wildly calling for help. Others clung to window ledges until the unbearable heat forced them to jump to their deaths. The Joelma Building had been built with little thought for fire precautions. As a result, 227 people lost their lives.

ROME BURNS

In Ancient Rome, the poor lived in multistory structures called *insulae*. These ramshackle wooden buildings caught fire easily, and there were at least three large fires in the city every day.

In A.D. 64, a blaze started among some shops. A Roman writer named Tacitus described how the fire "broke out, instantly gathered strength, and, driven by the wind, swept down the length of the Circus [or avenue]."

The emperor, Nero, returned from abroad when the flames threatened his own palace. He ordered food to be sent from neighboring towns and put up shelters for the homeless. After nine days the blaze ended, and Nero ordered the rebuilding of the city.

▼ *According to legend, Nero calmly played music and sang while Rome burned.*

The streets were made wider to stop fire from spreading so easily, and an enormous palace called the Golden House was built for the emperor. It had walls covered with jewels and a dining room with a revolving roof. It was rumored that Nero had planned the Great Fire himself—to make room for his grand new home.

▲ *A carving of Roman builders in about* A.D. *100. Nero started rebuilding Rome almost as soon as the Great Fire was put out.*

THE LIBRARY MYSTERY

The Ancient Egyptian city of Alexandria was famous for its magnificent library, which contained over half a million scrolls. It is a mystery what happened to the library: some writers in ancient times even claimed it was destroyed in 47 B.C.—in a fire started by the Roman general Julius Caesar.

▶ *Nobody knows for certain what happened to the Library of Alexandria, but it was probably destroyed by fire.*

SENGHENYDD COAL MINE

▲ *The people of Senghenydd gather at the mouth of the burning mine.*

In 1901, 81 miners were killed in a fire in the Senghenydd coal mine in Great Britain. Unfortunately, 12 years later there was an even greater tragedy.

On the morning of October 14, 1913, a massive explosion deep in the mine shook the whole town of Senghenydd. The blast was heard 11 miles (17 km) away in Cardiff.

Imagine the horror beneath the ground. Miners felt the ground shake as if there was an earthquake. Thick dust and poisonous fumes turned the air black. The miners could no longer see or breathe. The only light came from the raging fires that began to destroy the wooden props holding up the tunnels.

◄ *Twisted machinery at the mine entrance shows the force of the explosion.*

▼ *Miners' wives and children wait for news.*

The giant fans that normally blew life-giving air through the mine now spread the deadly flames. Rescuers were lowered into the mine, but they found many tunnels blocked by walls of fire.

The lives of 439 miners were lost in the underground fire at Senghenydd. It was the worst disaster in the history of British mining.

▲ *Crowds near Berlin stare at the metal skeleton of* Zeppelin L2, *all that remains after the airship exploded into flames.*

▼ *A rescue party comes up from the burning mine at Senghenydd.*

UNLUCKY 13

October 1913 was an extremely unlucky month for fires. On October 9, 1913, 122 people were drowned after the ship SS *Volturno* caught fire in the Atlantic. Next came the Senghenydd disaster. Finally, on October 17, 1913, the world's biggest airship, *Zeppelin L2*, exploded in a ball of flames, killing the 28-member crew.

GREAT CHICAGO FIRE

After 14 weeks of drought in the summer of 1871, fires were breaking out all over the Midwest [of the United States.] On the night of Sunday, October 8, two of the worst blazes in history took place.

People believe the Great Chicago Fire started when a cow kicked over a lantern in a barn that belonged to Mrs. Kate O'Leary. A fierce wind spread the flames. Houses, wooden sidewalks, grassy streets, and even the greasy surface of the river caught fire.

▶ *A newspaper seller cries out news of the Chicago disaster.*

▼ *Boats gather on Lake Michigan as Chicago blazes.*

▲ *Fire swept through San Francisco in 1906, after the city had been rocked by a huge earthquake.*

One survivor, 13-year-old Bessie Bradwell, recalled sparks filling the sky: "It was like a snowstorm, only the flakes were red instead of white." The fire left Chicago a smoldering ruin, with 250 dead. But the city would be rebuilt and would have the world's first skyscrapers.

Strangely, a forest fire began at the same moment in Wisconsin. It became a burning tornado so terrifying that some people took their own lives as it raced toward them. The town of Peshtigo was consumed in under an hour, and over 1,000 people died in the blazing forests.

EARTHQUAKE FIRES

There have been many city fires, and some of the worst have been caused by earthquakes. In the United States, fires destroyed 28,000 buildings after the 1906 San Francisco earthquake. In Japan in 1923, earthquakes followed by fires claimed the lives of over 140,000 people in the cities of Tokyo and Yokohama.

COCOANUT GROVE NIGHTCLUB

The Cocoanut Grove nightclub's windows were boarded up. Emergency doors were hidden behind curtains. Silk drapes hung from the ceiling, and papier-mâché palm trees stood among the tables. It was the perfect fire trap.

▲ *Crowds gather outside the Cocoanut Grove, as the victims of the fire are carried out into the street to wait for ambulances.*

Worst of all, on Saturday, November 28, 1942, the club in Boston, Massachusetts, was packed. The owner, a gangster named Barney Welansky, did not take heed of rules. He had a licence for only 460 occupants, but soldiers on leave from World War II had swelled the crowd to over a thousand.

◀ *Firefighters battle through the crowds to the blazing nightclub.*

18

THE IROQUOIS THEATRE

In the United States, fire laws for clubs and theaters were introduced after a blaze at the Iroquois Theatre, Chicago, on New Year's Eve of 1903. The blaze started on stage when a light set fire to scenery. Over 600 people were killed, 400 of them crushed in the panic to escape.

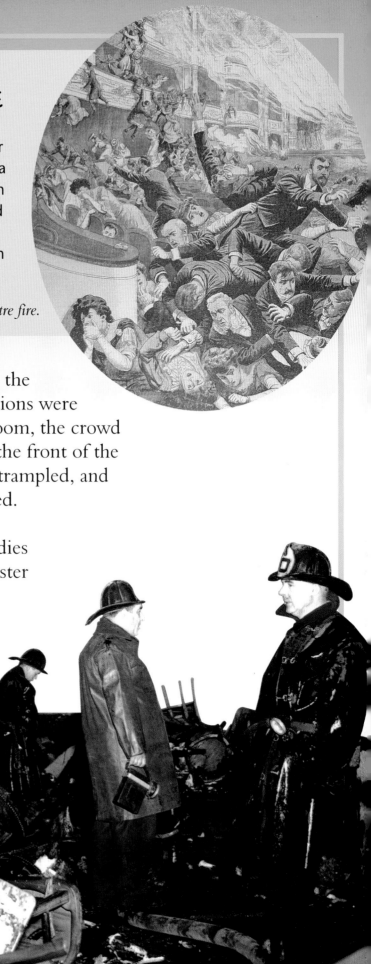

▶ *A painting, from 1904, of the Iroquois Theatre fire.*

A stray match probably started the fire in the Cocoanut Grove. In seconds, the decorations were ablaze. As thick, black smoke filled the room, the crowd stampeded toward the revolving door at the front of the club. In the panic, people were crushed, trampled, and suffocated—and part of the floor collapsed.

When firefighters arrived, they found bodies piled six deep. The Cocoanut Grove disaster had claimed the lives of 492 party-goers. The tragedy was a terrible lesson in the need to obey fire laws in clubs and theaters.

▶ *Officials inspect the blackened remains of the Cocoanut Grove.*

PIPER ALPHA OIL RIG

The Piper Alpha oil rig stood in the North Sea, 125 miles (200 km) off the coast of Scotland. At 9:45 P.M. on July 6, 1988, workers on the rig heard a sound like a woman screaming.

The sound was in fact made by leaking gas, which exploded into flames minutes later. The flames grew huge, feeding on the tons of oil being pumped into the rig. Gas pipes burst in the heat, and Piper Alpha became cloaked in blazing gas.

▼ *Piper Alpha blazes. The heat from the fire was so great it melted the decks of rescue ships.*

As the rig began to buckle and melt, men escaped the inferno by leaping into the icy seas. Helicopters and boats rescued what survivors they could but were driven back by the searing heat.

The blaze killed 167 men. Many were trapped in a housing unit built directly above the oil pipes. A survivor described the unit as "a hotel sitting on a potential fire bomb." A report written 12 months before had warned of the dangers of fire on Piper Alpha. Like so many fire disasters, this one could have been prevented.

◀ *A survivor of the Piper Alpha disaster returns to the mainland, lucky to be alive.*

▶ *In 1991, burning oil wells lit up Kuwait.*

A COUNTRY BURNS

In March 1991, at the end of the Gulf War, it seemed as if the whole of Kuwait was on fire. Troops from Iraq had set fire to 800 of Kuwait's oil wells. So much smoke filled the sky that black rain fell. It took eight months for firefighters to put out the blazes.

GREAT SURVIVORS

Fire disasters leave behind a tragic trail of death and destruction. But they also leave us some extraordinary tales of survival.

During the Australian bush fires in 1983, one family survived the flames by crouching inside a water tank. As the fires swept past, the water rose almost to boiling point. Some people survived the 1942 Cocoanut Grove nightclub fire by shutting themselves in a refrigerator.

Many survivors owe their lives to the efforts of firefighters. In recent years, American firefighters have made heroic rescues after terrorist attacks at the Federal Building in Oklahoma City and the World Trade Center in New York.

▲ *Three-year-old Brandon Denny, who survived a bomb explosion on April 19, 1995 in Oklahoma City. He heads home after spending over 100 days in hospital.*

▼ *A firefighter in the ruins of the World Trade Center in New York, USA. Firefighters saved many lives before the blazing buildings collapsed, killing over 3,000 people.*

In the Senghenydd disaster, 18 miners were rescued from the mine 16 hours after the fires began. There was an even greater escape in 1972, after fire raged through an American silver mine at Kellogg, Idaho. Only two out of 93 miners survived the blaze. Tom Wilkenson and Ron Flory escaped to the lower levels of the mine while the fire raged above them. They were eventually rescued – after spending a week in total darkness, 1500m below the ground.

▲ *Tom Wilkenson and Ron Flory, who survived a week below ground after the Kellogg silver mine fire.*

HIGH-WIRE HERO

At the Joelma Building fire in 1974, ropes were thrown across from a neighbouring building to help people escape. One firefighter, José Rufino, carried 18 people to safety by crawling across the ropes. Rufino was lucky to survive after being struck by a body falling from the building.

FIGHTING FIRES

Today, teams of firefighters are equipped with fire-resistant clothing and breathing masks. Fire engines with high-powered hoses are used to fight city fires. Forest fires can be tackled by aircraft loaded with water.

Firefighting has a long history. At the time of the Great Fire in A.D. 64, Rome already had its own fire brigade. Firefighters known as *vigiles* patrolled the streets, fighting fires with water buckets and blankets soaked in vinegar. They even used simple, wheeled fire engines.

▲ *In Argentina in 1998, a helicopter drops 264 gallons (1,000 liters) of water on a fire.*

HELL-FIGHTERS

After the 1988 Piper Alpha fire, a famous Texan firefighter named Red Adair put out the fires that blazed from the pipes pumping oil into the rig. He and his workers, known as hell-fighters, were paid $3 million (£2 million) for their work.

▲ *Red Adair, at the age of 76, tackles a fire in Kuwait.*

The Great Fire of London in 1666 was fought by bucket brigades, passing pails of water. Long rakes were used to pull down burning thatch from roofs, and water was pumped by "squirts"—which were like giant water pistols. By the time of the 1871 Great Chicago Fire, horse-drawn fire engines had steam-powered pumps.

Many historical fires might have been put out if they had been tackled sooner. Perhaps the biggest improvement in firefighting is in communication. Fire alarms and emergency telephone numbers mean that firefighters now reach blazes within minutes of their starting.

▲ You can almost feel the heat from this forest fire, in California in the summer of 1989.

DISASTER FACTS

An 18th-century painting of the Great Fire of Rome. Some Roman writers claimed that Nero's soldiers beat up anyone who tried to put out the blaze.

CANNON FIRE

On June 29, 1613, during a performance of Shakespeare's play *Henry VIII* at the Globe Theatre in London, a cannon was fired on stage. Its cannonball landed in the Globe's thatched roof and started a fire that destroyed the entire theatre.

BOOK BURNING

In 1666, most printers worked in London. So the Great Fire destroyed large numbers of precious books, including many of the original copies of William Shakespeare's plays.

FLAME BLAME

After a major fire, people always look for somebody to blame. Nero blamed Christians for the Fire of Rome in A.D. 64 and used it as an excuse to torture them. Some people claimed that Catholics had started the Great Fire of London in 1666.

VIGILANT VIGILES

The *vigiles* of Ancient Rome had to do more than just fight fires. They were expected to chase escaped slaves and look after people's towels when they were bathing.

LUCKY O'LEARY

Mrs. O'Leary's cow might have started the Great Chicago Fire of 1871, but because the wind was blowing in the other direction, Mrs. O'Leary's house escaped the flames.

FIRE RATS

In the 1800s, a number of fires in London were caused by rats chewing through gas pipes or gnawing at the ends of matches.

DIRTY RATS

After the Iroquois Theatre blaze of 1903, Chicago undertakers cashed in by raising their prices.

FIRE INSURANCE

After the 1906 San Francisco earthquake, many people claimed their buildings had been destroyed by fire—because their insurance did not cover them for earthquakes.

SMOKE ALARM

Forest fires in Indonesia in 1997–1998 filled the capital city, Jakarta, with thick smoke. People could not see farther than 50 feet (15 m), and breathing in the smoke was the same as smoking 600 cigarettes a day.

▼ *Smoke billows from the fires that followed the 1906 San Francisco earthquake.*

DISASTER WORDS

Airship (AIR-ship) A balloon that can be steered and was once a popular form of aircraft.

Brimstone (BRIM-STONE) Another word for sulphur, which is a substance that burns easily. Brimstone was believed to keep the fires of hell burning.

Bush fire (BUSH FIRE) The name for an uncontrolled fire in the countryside, especially in Australia.

Crystal Palace (KRISS-tuhl PAL-iss) A famous building of iron and glass that was built in London in 1851 to hold an event called the Great Exhibition.

Drought (DROUT) A period of dry weather, when there is no rain. Drought dries out the land, making it easy for fires to start.

Eucalyptus (yoo-kuh-LIP-tuhss) A tall evergreen tree that grows in Australia.

Fire precautions (FIRE pri-KAW-shuhns) Actions taken to try to prevent fires, such as providing fire exits, alarms, and sprinklers.

Fire-resistant (FIRE-ri-ZISS-tuhnss) Something that does not catch fire, even when placed in flames.

▼ *The Crystal Palace in Hyde Park, 1851, during the Great Exhibition. In 1852, the entire building was moved to nearby Sydenham. It burnt down in 1936, after a fire so hot the windows exploded.*

Gulf War (GUHLF WAR) The war fought against Iraq in 1991 by a group of countries led by the United States, after Iraq had invaded the neighboring country of Kuwait in 1990.

Today, many people live and work in skyscrapers like these in Hong Kong. It is difficult to fight fires when they break out in such tall buildings.

Inferno (in-FUR-noh) A scene of horror that seems like hell, particularly a terrible fire.

Meteor (MEE-tee-ur) A mass of rock or metal that falls toward Earth from outer space. Most meteors burn up in the sky before they reach Earth.

Middle East (MID-uhl EEST) A region of southwestern Asia.

Oil rig (OIL RIG) A platform used for drilling oil.

Prehistoric (pree-hi-STOR-ik) Ancient, before history was written down.

Ramshackle (RAM-shak-uhl) Carelessly constructed, rickety, unstable.

Scrolls (SKROHLS) Rolls of paper or parchment, which people in ancient times used in the same way as we use books.

York Minster (YORK MIN-stur) A cathedral in the city of York, in England.

DISASTER PROJECTS

CITY HISTORY

Choose a city, then try to find out about the biggest fires in that city's history. A large city like London, Chicago, or Tokyo will have many major fires to investigate. You might be able to find out about modern fires by looking in old newspapers, which you can find in some libraries. Use reference books and websites to find pictures of fires that you can copy and stories told by witnesses. You might be able to copy old maps of the city, to show how they changed after major fires.

FIRE SAFETY

Prepare a project on fire safety. Where is your nearest fire station? How many firefighters do they have, and do these firefighters have other jobs? What equipment does the fire station have? How do people get help when there is a fire? How does your school keep you safe from fire? You can find information in your school, local library, and fire station.

▼ *Panic during the 1871 Great Fire of Chicago. The fire changed the entire history of the city.*

▲ *Firefighters battle a blaze in September 2001 at a museum in Massachusetts.*

FIRE TIMELINE

Make a list of all the fire disasters you have found out about, and put them in the order that they happened. Use reference books and websites to find the dates of other important fires. Make a wall chart. Put the dates in order down the left-hand side and the descriptions of the fires on the right. Decorate it with pictures of the most important fires.

 FIRE WEBSITES

www.chicagohs.org/fire
Excellent pictures and eyewitness accounts of the 1871 Great Fire of Chicago.

www.fire.org.uk
About the fire service in Great Britain, with links to lots of good historical sites.

www.fema.gov/kids/wldfire
A cartoon crab gives you a guided tour of fire safety! A fun site with some good photographs.

http://home.earthlink.net/~wroush/disasters/index.html
A good starting point: a timeline showing major disasters of the 20th century.

INDEX

©Belitha Press Ltd. 2003